31

METHAMPHETAMINE AND ITS DANGERS

by Marty Erickson

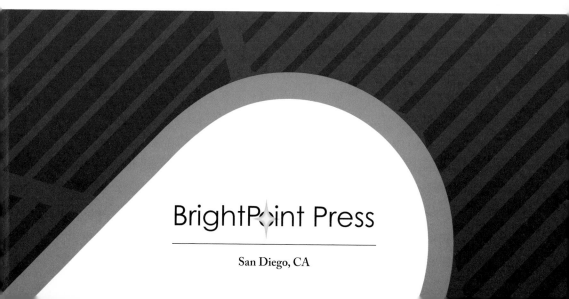

BrightPoint Press

San Diego, CA

BrightPoint Press

© 2020 BrightPoint Press
An imprint of ReferencePoint Press, Inc.
Printed in the United States

For more information, contact:
BrightPoint Press
PO Box 27779
San Diego, CA 92198
www.BrightPointPress.com

OCT 0 2 2019

LIBRARY OF CONGRESS CATALOGING-IN-PUBLICATION DATA

Names: Erickson, Marty, 1991- author.
Title: Methamphetamine and its dangers / Marty Erickson.
Description: San Diego, CA : ReferencePoint Press, Inc., [2020] | Series:
  Drugs and their dangers | Audience: Grades 9 to 12. | Includes
  bibliographical references and index.
Identifiers: LCCN 2019003225 (print) | LCCN 2019007410 (ebook) | ISBN
  9781682827123 (ebook) | ISBN 9781682827116 (hardcover)
Subjects: LCSH: Methamphetamine abuse--Juvenile literature. |
  Methamphetamine--Juvenile literature. | Drug abuse--Juvenile literature.
Classification: LCC RC568.A45 (ebook) | LCC RC568.A45 E75 2020 (print) | DDC
  362.29/95--dc23
LC record available at https://lccn.loc.gov/2019003225

CONTENTS

FACT SHEET

- Methamphetamine is an addictive stimulant.

- Meth can cause teeth to rot. It can also cause infections.

- Users may experience memory loss. Most of the effects on the brain eventually go away.

- Areas with meth labs usually experience higher crime rates.

- Meth labs may explode. The ingredients are very dangerous.

- Withdrawal lasts approximately two weeks.

- The most effective way to get sober is to attend a treatment program.

- Law enforcement agencies are trying new ways to reduce the number of drug arrests. They are using different methods rather than sending people to jail.

A TOUGH ADDICTION

Carren Clem was the daughter of a police officer. She knew drugs were dangerous. Her dad worked on the drug force. But Carren was struggling. She had been raped three years earlier, and she didn't know how to cope with her depression. Carren tried methamphetamine for the first time in high school.

Methamphetamine users will do almost anything to get a fix.

After that first high, she became

addicted. She did almost anything to get

more drugs. She said, "I would do anything

with anyone to get drugs—steal car stereos,

Most users go through bad situations before getting help.

have sex, whatever. Often when I woke

up I didn't know where I was or how I

had gotten there."[1] Meth was taking over

Carren's life.

Meth causes feelings of joy. But when the high wears off, users often feel sad and hopeless. Thoughts of suicide are common. That's what happened to Carren. When she told her friends about her feelings, they didn't help her. They gave her more drugs. Carren tried to kill herself, but she didn't die.

She knew something had to change. Carren called her youth pastor. The youth pastor and Carren's parents got her into a treatment center. Treatment wasn't easy, but Carren was able to get **sober**. Today, she works at a fitness center. She is married and has a daughter.

Methamphetamine is a highly addictive drug. People who try meth have a hard time stopping. Meth causes many physical and mental health issues. Illegal meth use harms communities in lots of ways. Getting help for addiction is possible but can be hard. Sobriety is important to begin healing the damage the drug use caused.

Many users find support groups helpful for quitting.

CHAPTER ONE

WHAT IS METHAMPHETAMINE?

Methamphetamine is a stimulant. It is called meth for short. It is also called other names. They include chalk, crank, crystal, ice, and speed. Some of these names come from its appearance. Meth is usually sold as a powder or pill. Often, the drug is white or blue. Meth tastes bitter. Users can smoke, swallow

Meth is often in crystal form.

pills, or snort powder. They may also inject

the drug.

Meth has been around for more than

one hundred years. Meth is related to the

drug amphetamine. Amphetamine was discovered in the late 1800s. Doctors used it as medicine. Meth is a kind of amphetamine. It was developed in 1893 in Japan. A plant in Asia contains a chemical called ephedrine. People in China, Japan, and Pakistan used its leaves. They made tea with them. The tea helped with asthma and colds. This plant is the base for all amphetamines.

HISTORY OF METH

People used amphetamines legally in the early 1900s. They could be bought over the counter. The drugs were used as diet pills.

But doctors realized how addictive they could be. By the 1980s, some people were illegally making meth at home. Homes that make meth are called meth labs. They are very toxic and dangerous. The US government passed new laws in the 1980s. These laws regulated certain

METH USE AROUND THE WORLD

Meth isn't only used in the United States. Use in the United States and Europe has decreased. But other areas are seeing an increase. Southeast Asia has seen a large jump in meth use.

Some ingredients found in medications are regulated. They are used to produce meth illegally.

meth ingredients. This lowered meth
production. But more people started
bringing meth into the country. In the
twenty-first century, meth is illegal except in
a few cases.

MEDICAL USES

Doctors can prescribe a low-dose meth
pill. It can be used to treat obesity. Low
doses can lessen a person's appetite.
The drug can also treat attention-deficit
hyperactivity disorder (ADHD). It helps the
person remain focused. Some researchers
are testing meth to treat other conditions.
Narcolepsy causes a patient to fall asleep

without warning. Researchers are looking into meth as a solution. Doctors believe low doses could keep patients awake.

MAKING METH

"Meth is strikingly easy to make," says anthropologist Jason Pine.[2] He studies the effect of meth labs on small towns. Some meth is brought into the United States from other countries. There are large labs in Mexico. Labs can produce many pounds of meth every day. Most labs in the United Sates are in houses. People who make meth are called cooks. The places where they cook are sometimes called kitchens. Cooks can create a batch of meth in two days. But there is a simpler method called "shake and bake." It takes only a couple minutes.

The ingredients for meth are toxic. Ephedrine is the main ingredient. Some cold medicines and diet pills use ephedrine. High doses of it cause heart problems.

Other ingredients include **lye** and hydrochloric acid. These materials are **corrosive**. Hydrochloric acid can strip rust from steel. Boiling hydrochloric acid makes meth crystalize. The acidic gas reacts with the other chemicals. It creates a solid that is white or clear.

The "shake and bake" method is simpler. All of the ingredients are poured into a soda bottle. Users shake the bottle until crystals form. But these chemicals react dangerously when mixed. Sometimes cooks open the bottle too quickly.

Meth labs have lots of dangerous chemicals. Cleaning houses that had labs requires special gear.

The mixture explodes. The acidic ingredients leave serious chemical burns.

Shake and bake accidents can happen without warning. Sergeant Erik Eidsen works with the Missouri Highway Patrol. He explains, "At some point, someone has to 'burp' the bottle or loosen the cap to let out gas, and if it isn't done right, it'll explode."[3] The fire burns quickly. Users sometimes make the meth in their cars. If something happens, users may not have time to escape. Vehicles can explode if the fire reaches the gas tank.

The shake and bake method for making meth can be done anywhere, even in a car. It is a dangerous process and can set the car on fire.

METHAMPHETAMINE USE IN WORLD WAR II

Soldiers around the world used meth during World War II (1939–1945). Meth is a stimulant. Soldiers used the drug to stay awake. German officials ordered 35 million tablets of meth for soldiers before invading France.

Shake and bake and traditional methods differ in the amount of ingredients needed. In typical kitchens, cooks need lots of ephedrine. Shake and bake doesn't need as much. One box of cold medicine is enough for several batches. This method produces a stronger drug. It is less expensive and harder to track. All of the

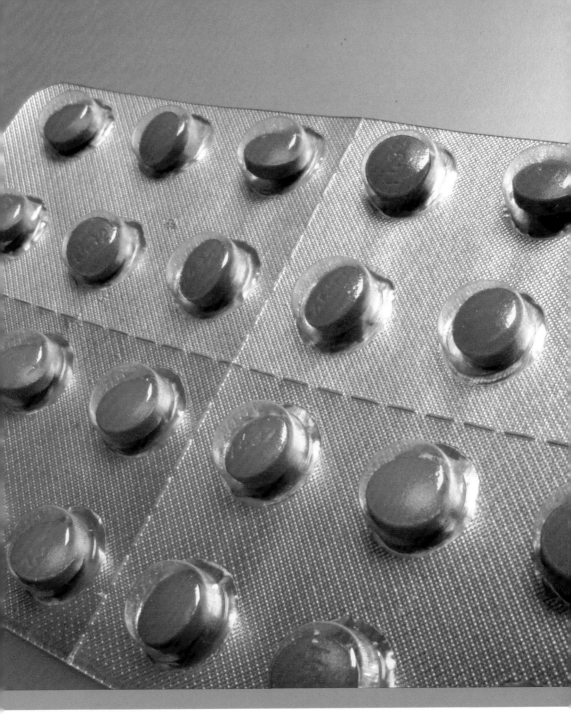

Drugstores track the sales of medications with ephedrine. This helps law enforcement catch meth cooks.

Meth lab fires are very dangerous because of the chemical fumes.

ingredients are easy to find. They aren't

regulated. Cooks don't have to buy a large

amount of any one chemical. This means

police have a harder time finding labs.

Making meth is very dangerous.

Explosions happen. This is a common way

the police find out about meth labs.

CHAPTER TWO

HOW DOES METHAMPHETAMINE AFFECT THE BODY?

Meth affects the body in many ways. Most short-term effects happen in the brain. But the drug also causes long-term changes to the body.

When people take meth, they experience a high. Meth affects the reward centers of the brain. "Meth excites . . . the brain

When meth is inhaled, the effects on the brain are almost immediate.

function that causes pleasure . . . from the

anticipation of reward," says Jason Pine.[4]

A large amount of dopamine is released.

Dopamine is a chemical that makes people feel happy. This feeling of happiness makes people want to keep using the drug. But the more a person uses meth, the more likely they are to become addicted.

A person who takes meth experiences other effects too. They will feel more alert. It will be easier for them to concentrate. One journalist described her sister's meth use. She said her sister "had to be on the computer. . . . Then computers faded, and she was obsessed with diving into dumpsters."[5] People may take many doses of meth for days in a row.

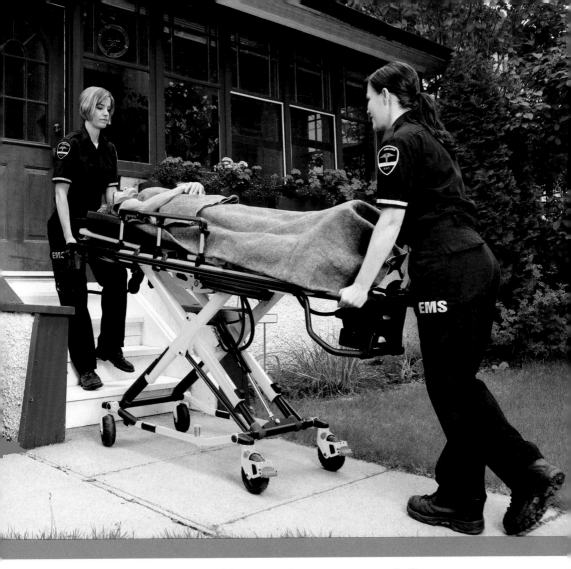

Meth use can lead to overdose or organ failure. Both of these can kill the user.

They continue to experience a high. Meth

decreases appetite. During a high, users

will experience faster breathing. Their heart

Coming down from meth is hard for users. This is only the beginning of the negative effects on the body.

rate increases. Their blood pressure goes up. Body temperature increases as well.

People can overdose on meth. An overdose can cause heart attack and stroke. But people may also experience organ failure. When the body gets too hot, the liver and kidneys begin to shut down. They can't filter out the toxins from meth.

THE HIGHS AND LOWS

Methamphetamine highs can last four to twelve hours. Afterward, a user will experience a comedown. As the effects of meth wear off, people experience different symptoms. Many feel depressed and anxious. They become sleepy. They have low energy. Depression, anxiety, and sleep issues all come from a lack of dopamine. Users may also have muscle pain and headaches.

TOLL ON THE BODY

To avoid these effects, people continue to use meth. But meth itself takes a heavy toll on the body. People who use the drug suffer many medical issues. Many users have dental problems. But these issues are worse than just bad breath. Meth affects blood flow. With lower blood flow, teeth begin to decay. "Meth mouth" describes

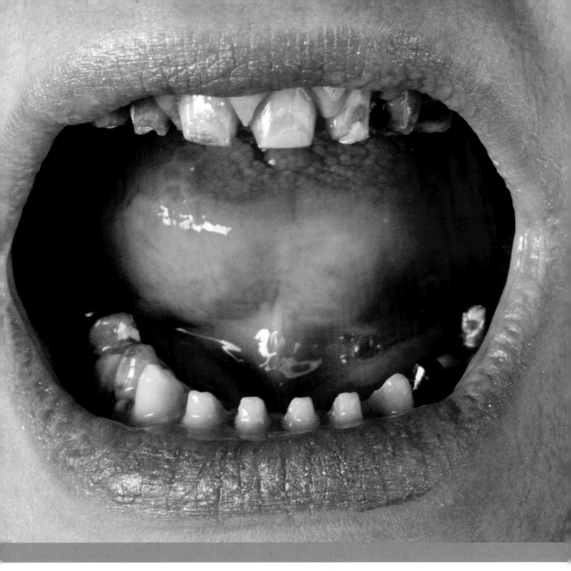

Smoking meth rots users' teeth. The teeth can get infected.

this problem. Teeth can turn black. They

might fall out on their own. Dentists

may also need to remove rotting teeth.

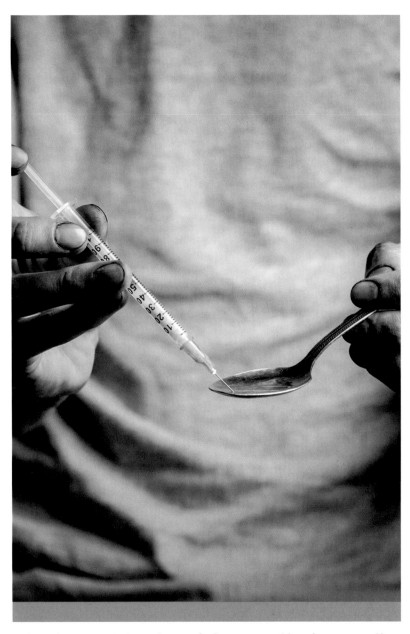

Injecting meth has lots of dangers. Sharing needles can lead to diseases, and dull needles cause large bruises and scars.

One study showed that 96 percent of people who used meth had cavities. Thirty-one percent of users lost six or more teeth.

People who use meth lose weight. They may look like they have an eating disorder. Meth also causes people to age more quickly. Their skin loses its ability to stretch. This causes wrinkles to form. Researchers have found that meth users appear to age ten times faster than nonusers.

Users' cuts take a long time to heal. This can pose other risks. An injury that takes longer to heal is more likely to become infected. Meth users may have a harder time fighting off those infections.

Users who inject meth are vulnerable to diseases. They are more likely to contract blood-borne infections. These include hepatitis and HIV. They are serious illnesses by themselves. Fighting infection and addiction at the same time can be hard.

LONG-TERM EFFECTS

Long-term use impacts memory and concentration. Many users report being unable to follow verbal instructions.

Even if a person stops using meth, he will still experience lasting effects. Many former

Meth has lasting effects on the body. Paranoia can last even after users quit.

PARKINSON'S DISEASE

Parkinson's disease affects a person's brain. The part of the brain that Parkinson's damages is the same part of the brain that meth affects. One doctor said meth users were up to three times more likely to develop Parkinson's than nonusers.

users report a lasting feeling of paranoia.

They feel like people are watching them. Or

they may feel like they are in danger. This

feeling has to do with the damage meth

did to their brains. Over time, those feelings

go away.

Long-term effects last for months. They may even last years after people stop using meth. Doctors say that the brain can heal. But that can take more than a year. Some brain functions will not go back to the way they were prior to meth use.

Former meth users may also **hallucinate**. They see things that

METH BUGS

Some people who take meth think they see bugs. The bugs crawl under their skin. Users scratch their arms and legs. They try to get the bugs out of their bodies. Many users get scabs and sores. These sores can get infected if they are not cleaned well.

aren't there. They may see objects or people. But in reality, there isn't anything in the room. One user reported running away from a hallucination for hours. He said, "I was awake for a month straight. My mind didn't have a chance to rest and be able to tell what was real and what wasn't."[6]

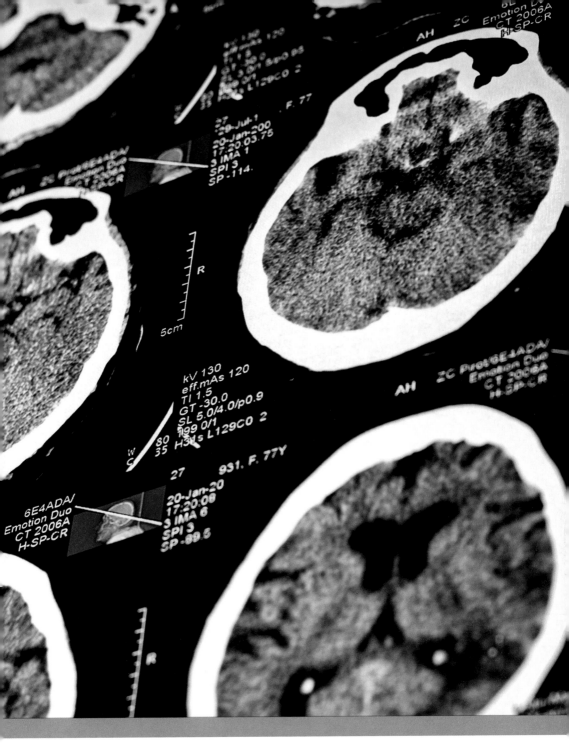

Meth damages the brain. The damage can have a lasting effect on the user.

CHAPTER THREE

HOW DOES METHAMPHETAMINE AFFECT SOCIETY?

Most meth in the United States is made in homes. They are often called meth labs. These labs are not scientific. The cooks are not scientists. The ingredients are available at any grocery store. Some people buy equipment like

Most meth labs are in homes. Labs can contaminate the whole house.

beakers and burners. But making meth in a

house requires only a kitchen.

DANGERS OF COOKING METH

Ingredients for meth are toxic on their own. When they mix together, they become even more dangerous. There isn't a set recipe. Cooks each have their own list of ingredients. Some include gasoline and lighter fluid. Chemicals interact harshly.

They can explode if cooks aren't careful.

Many cooks do not protect themselves.

Some may even be high while they are

making meth.

The ingredients in meth smell bad. The

fumes from making meth are dangerous.

Many meth houses try to vent some of the

gases out. But even a small amount can

make people sick.

Making meth creates a lot of waste. Meth

is made from liquids. But in its final form,

it is a solid. Not all of the liquid gets turned

into a solid. Making 1 pound (0.5 kg) of

meth creates 5 pounds (2.3 kg) of waste.

Waste chemicals are toxic and can kill plants and grass.

Waste is poured down kitchen sinks. It enters the drinking supply. Sometimes, cooks pour the waste in the yard. It enters the ground. Waste kills plants. It can remain in the ground for several years.

It can be hard to tell a meth lab from a regular house. Meth labs are often discovered after accidents. The chemicals can start fires or explode. Firefighters are called to the homes. Meth cooks and firefighters are burned from the chemicals and the fire.

Explosions are dangerous for cooks and people nearby. Lab chemicals are fuel for the fire. Many of the chemicals are explosive. They catch fire easily. These explosions can damage neighbors' houses. Fires spread. Flying debris breaks windows.

Meth labs aren't only dangerous when they explode. Fumes escape through windows and doors. If kids breathe in the gases, they can become sick. One couple in Utah got sick from the fumes. They had to have sinus surgery. When their son was born, he had lung problems. He stopped breathing. He spent time in the hospital but lived.

CRIME AFFECTS A COMMUNITY

Areas with meth labs have higher rates of car theft. This increase in crime is dangerous for families nearby. They may not know the reason for the increase in crime. Anthropologist Jason Pine says, "Many meth cooks are repeat offenders. While at home awaiting trial . . . they may be busted for manufacturing yet again."[7]

Meth users cost a community in even more ways too. Many wind up in prison. Their time in prison also costs taxpayers. If they need special medical care from meth use, the costs are even higher.

SENTENCING

Drug offenders receive long prison sentences. Many are the result of mandatory minimum laws. Mandatory minimums mean that prison sentences have to be a certain length of time. Depending on the amount, meth can carry a five-year minimum sentence for a first offense. A second offense can require a twenty-year

Mandatory minimum sentences take the sentencing role out of the judge's hands.

sentence. One man was sentenced to forty

years in prison. He was a first-time offender.

But because he was working with another

Users who go to prison are more likely to be arrested again.

person who used weapons, he got a longer sentence.

People in favor of prison reform argue that mandatory minimums put a strain on the prison system. Prisoners are held for many years. When they are released, many have a hard time finding jobs. Some jobs have rules against hiring people who have been in prison. But this means many former users and dealers go back to making and selling drugs. It is the only way they can support themselves. This creates a cycle. Drug use leads to crime. Crime leads to more arrests. More offenses lead to

longer sentences.

Most drug offenders are not violent.

Many believe offenders would do better

in a treatment program. One study found

that releasing the 39 percent of the prison

population that was nonviolent could save

the United States $20 billion each year.

Many prison reform supporters believe users would do better in rehab than jail. This could potentially save the United States billions of dollars every year.

CHAPTER FOUR

WHAT ARE THE TREATMENTS FOR METHAMPHETAMINE ABUSE?

Meth is highly addictive. Its effects make it pleasant to use. They also make it hard to quit. Staying off of meth can be difficult.

Withdrawal symptoms are similar to comedown effects. They begin within a day

It is hard for addicted users to quit.

of quitting. People who are addicted rely on

the drug. Their bodies need it. Withdrawal

is the body's reaction to not having it

anymore. Symptoms of withdrawal include

Users are often nauseated during withdrawal. They may have many other symptoms.

many unpleasant effects. Some of them

can even be dangerous.

Symptoms depend on how addicted a

person is to meth. The more time a person

spent using meth, the harder it will be to

quit. There are physical and mental effects

of withdrawal. Physical symptoms include

cravings, **fatigue**, nausea, chills, and

shaking. People who are in withdrawal will

want to take meth. They know meth would

stop the symptoms. Withdrawal patients

sleep a lot. Sleep is the best way for a body

to heal. Patients also have psychological

symptoms. They may be anxious

and depressed. Some imagine bugs under their skin. These symptoms last about two weeks. This is one of the reasons it's so hard to quit. Staying clean can be hard. One woman in Iowa was interviewed after being sober for sixty-three days. She said she still wanted to do meth. In an interview she said, "I'm so scared. . . . It's such a strong pull, such an addiction."[8]

Medications are available to help during the withdrawal from some drugs. But meth isn't one of them. However, medication can help with some symptoms. **Detoxing** can be a challenge. It is best to go to a treatment center. Treatment centers have experts. These professionals can help patients with feelings of depression and anxiety.

TREATMENT CENTERS

Treatment centers also provide support for people who are addicted. Being with other

DIFFERENT KINDS OF REHAB CENTERS

There are two types of treatment programs. Long-term programs create a community. Patients stay in these residential programs for months. They meet with counselors and live with other patients. Short-term programs usually last three to six weeks. Patients in these programs live at home.

In counseling, former users learn how to handle cravings. They also learn how to change bad habits that lead to drug use.

people in treatment is helpful. A community

can help someone stay sober. Some people

use Cognitive Behavioral Therapy (CBT).

CBT teaches how to cope with cravings. Patients learn to change their behavior. CBT is often done in a group setting. This allows patients to share their challenges with each other. One woman attended a treatment center. She wrote about her success. She said, "After twenty-six years of meth addiction I'm approaching my two-year clean date."[9]

Many organizations have hotlines. Drug users can call these phone numbers. They can speak with a counselor. They can get help or resources to get sober. Some sites also have instant messaging available.

Hotlines can help users and former users who are struggling with addiction.

These services save lives. Hotlines aren't just for people who want to get clean. They are helpful for people who are struggling to stay sober. The people who answer the phone give support to anyone who needs it.

PREVENTION PROGRAMS

Communities want to prevent meth addiction. One of the most successful federal programs tracked ingredients. Ephedrine is the main ingredient in meth. It is also in cold medicine. Many states passed laws that people must be eighteen years old to buy cold medicine. Officials keep track of how much a person buys.

Customers can only buy a certain amount every thirty days. Some states require patients to get a prescription to buy drugs like Sudafed. Sudafed's main ingredient is pseudoephedrine. Pseudoephedrine is similar to ephedrine. These laws sharply reduced the number of meth labs.

Some people believe that harsher punishments will help people stay away from meth. Scientists and mental health experts disagree. They say that it doesn't matter how long a prison sentence is. The thing that makes the biggest difference is how quickly consequences happen.

Some cities give police the option to arrest users or send them to treatment.

Waiting for trial and a sentence can take

months. Some communities are using

police to help change behavior. They believe

this works better than punishing drug users.

ENFORCEMENT ALTERNATIVES

The Law Enforcement Assisted Diversion (LEAD) program allows officers to make a choice. They can choose to arrest a drug user. Or they can connect that person with a case manager. The case manager finds a treatment program. LEAD started in Seattle, Washington, in 2011. Since then, it spread across the United States. Cities are seeing a change in drug use and drug-related crimes. Participants in LEAD are 58 percent less likely to start using again compared to the people who are arrested.

One key factor is how quickly consequences happen. A case manager contacts the user within a couple days. Police officers follow up with the case manager and the client. They want to make sure the person is doing well. Clients then are admitted into a treatment program.

LEAD PROGRAMS

LEAD programs are used in places such as King County, Washington. They are inspired by arrest referral programs in the United Kingdom. The King County program started in 2011. Oregon and New Mexico have also adopted LEAD programs.

In the program, they have more support than in prison. These therapy groups and counselors increase the chances that the clients will stay sober. With promising rehab options, many former users can find healthy lives. They can rejoin society and help build a better future.

With treatment many users can get clean. A good support system can help them build a better future.

GLOSSARY

addiction
dependence on a substance, thing, or activity

corrosive
eats away at another object

detox
the process of the body getting rid of a substance

fatigue
tiredness

hallucinate
to see something that isn't there

lye
a chemical used in making soap

Parkinson's disease
a disease that affects the brain; patients lose the ability to walk or hold things and have trouble remembering events

sober
no longer using drugs

withdrawal
the process of stopping taking a drug

SOURCE NOTES

INTRODUCTION: A TOUGH ADDICTION

1. Quoted in "Crystal Clear: Stories of People Who Faced Meth Addiction," *The Recovery Village*, n.d. www.therecoveryvillage.com.

CHAPTER ONE: WHAT IS METHAMPHETAMINE?

2. Quoted in Clay Cansler, "Making Sense of Making Meth," *Distillations*, 2015. www.sciencehistory.org.

3. Quoted in Doming Ramirez Jr, "'Shake-and-Bake' Meth Could Have Explosive Consequences," *Seattle Times*, September 15, 2013. www.seattletimes.com.

CHAPTER TWO: HOW DOES METHAMPHETAMINE AFFECT THE BODY?

4. Quoted in Cansler, "Making Sense of Making Meth."

5. Thea Singer, "Recipe for Disaster," *Washington Post*, January 15, 2006, www.washingtonpost.com.

6. Quoted in Emily Gallagher, "Paranoia and Hallucinations Just Part of the Horror of Methamphetamine," *Times West Virginian*, September 21, 2014. www.timeswv.com.

CHAPTER THREE: HOW DOES METHAMPHETAMINE AFFECT SOCIETY?

7. Quoted in Cansler, "Making Sense of Making Meth."

CHAPTER FOUR: WHAT ARE THE TREATMENTS FOR METHAMPHETAMINE ABUSE?

8. Quoted in Lee Rood, "Iowa Meth User Recounts Path of Addiction: 'I Lost Everything in 3 Years,'" *Des Moines Register*, May 18, 2018. www.desmoinesregister.com.

9. Quoted in "American Addiction Centers Reviews," *American Addiction Centers*, October 29, 2018. https://americanaddictioncenters.org.

FOR FURTHER RESEARCH

BOOKS

Hal Marcovitz, *The Dangers of Methamphetamine*. San Diego, CA: ReferencePoint Press, 2017.

Claudia Martin, *Drug Wars*. New York: Cavendish Square: 2018.

Nic and David Sheff, *High: Everything You Want to Know About Drugs, Alcohol, and Addiction*. Boston, MA: Houghton Mifflin Harcourt, 2018.

INTERNET SOURCES

"Methamphetamine (Meth)," *Nemours*, May 2018. https://kidshealth.org.

"Methamphetamine (Meth)," *NIDA for Teens*, March 2019. https://teens.drugabuse.gov.

"Methamphetamine (Meth)," *Partnership for Drug-Free Kids*, August 17, 2018. https://drugfree.org.

WEBSITES

American Addiction Centers
https://americanaddictioncenters.org

American Addiction Centers provides information and services to adults with drug abuse issues. They have different treatment options for patients.

The Meth Project
www.methproject.org

The Meth Project started in 2005. It works to reduce drug abuse. The Meth Project works on public education and outreach.

National Drug Hotline
http://drughelpline.org

The National Drug Hotline is an organization for people who struggle with drug addiction. They provide resources so people can get help.

INDEX

IMAGE CREDITS

ABOUT THE AUTHOR

Marty Erickson is a genderqueer writer living in Minnesota. Marty uses the pronouns "they/them/theirs." They write books for young people full time and like to go hiking.